Black Thoughts:
Emancipating Kevin X

Black Thoughts: Emancipating Kevin X

Written by: Kevin J. Alexander, Jr. X

Copyright © 2023 by Kevin J. Alexander, Jr. X.

Library of Congress Control Number:		2023905689
ISBN:	Hardcover	978-1-6698-7212-2
	Softcover	978-1-6698-7211-5
	eBook	978-1-6698-7210-8

All rights reserved. No part of this book may be reproduced or transmitted in any form or by any means, electronic or mechanical, including photocopying, recording, or by any information storage and retrieval system, without permission in writing from the copyright owner.

Any people depicted in stock imagery provided by Getty Images are models, and such images are being used for illustrative purposes only.
Certain stock imagery © Getty Images.

Print information available on the last page.

Rev. date: 04/17/2023

To order additional copies of this book, contact:
Xlibris
844-714-8691
www.Xlibris.com
Orders@Xlibris.com

851704

TABLE OF CONTENTS

Introduction vii
"Lord, I Need Your Help" 1
"One Mistake" 5
"Wake Me Up" 9
"I'm Addicted" 11
"Where Do People Go When They Die?" 13
"The Path to Redemption" 16
"Lord, I'm Undefeated" 19
"In the Prison of Unforgiveness" 22
"I wish" 24
"Don't Put More on Me Than I Can Bear" 25
"I Feel Like a Ghost" 27
"See the World Through My Eyes" 30
"On My Back" 36
"Don't Count Me Out" 40
"The Pain Won't Go Away" 42
"What Would It Be Like if You Were Here" 44
"You Wasn't There" 47
"My Story" 51
"Rain On Me" 54
"I Can't Breathe" 58
"Out of the Concrete a Rose Grew" 61
"Bridgett's Efflorescence" 64
Acknowledgements 67
About the Author 71

Introduction

I remember, after conviction and sentencing, being sent to Angola Prison. I was a 17-year-old boy. I was lost, afraid, and worried that this conviction and sentence had terminated my life as a free citizen. When I arrived, the Angola Administration processed me into the system. Classification officers, the people tasked with classifying where inmates would live, assigned me to live in a lockdown cell for 23 hours a day. The area I was assigned was called the Transitional Unit (TU). The TU environment housed all types of offenders; men convicted for murder, rape, armed robbery, and kidnapping. The list goes on forever.

When I came into the Department of Corrections, I faced so many fears and uncertainties. The most perpetual thought, and a constant nagging question most prisoners asked themselves, is "When am I going home?" All of us held these thoughts about time. Too many of us doing time never considered how precious our time is and the importance of using our time wisely until we acquired this sentence that required us to forcefully give our time to another –the system. This was our punishment for committing a crime! We wondered day and night when we would be free again. The awful thing about all of this, was losing the ability to have control over what I wanted to do and where I wanted to go. I gave this autonomy away to a system that would now dictate what I did or didn't do with my time. Now, in prison, someone else dictated where I would live and who I would live with for the next 32 years. Knowing this fact, completely stressed me out!

At that time, I had months before I turned 18-years-old. Honestly, being sentenced to 32 years in the Department of Corrections felt like eternity.

The problem I encountered with this entire lockdown situation, was having to live on a tier with 12 other "Lifers" (men who were serving life sentences for various crimes). We were all in one-man cells, with no access to socialize or mingle with other inmates. We only used the phone once a week for 15 minutes. The administration exiled me to the lockdown unit in the name of protecting me. Their logic was my age presented my danger. A seventeen-year-old convicted murderer IS danger! Straight bullshit! I was pissed off, nevertheless powerless about what I could do concerning this predicament because in actuality I couldn't do anything about it.

I resided on a tier, in a solitaire cell, with other men who were considered animals deserving to be in a cage. The security felt like we were untamable. Their best solution was to lock us up in cages, or so they thought. Some of these men were mentally inept or socially unstable. They were men who couldn't live in general population with other inmates. They were considered violent, a threat and danger to others as well as to themselves. All of these men had a story attached to their pain and hurt that not only physically incarcerated them, but spiritually and mentally incarcerated them. I struggled to adjust to living in a one-man cell the size of a janitor's closet. This adjustment became a constant threat to my mental health. This place was my new home according to the Department of Corrections.

This place was so disgusting and repulsive! It made me, a human being, feel like I was at a cemetery. Obviously, the difference was, these men were the walking dead! The Louisiana State Penitentiary is a world within a world, a city within a city. This place held the undefeated title for beating men down until their death. Cursing them to live in prison until they die. Angola was filthy with incarcerated souls who died fighting to get out of there. Some men were guilty, some were innocent. Some were illegally convicted –I would say 85% of them. These men fought for years litigating issues in their case. The judicial system would win the fight most of the time, legally or illegally. Angola is a place where convicted offenders do their time until it expires. Men face the consequences of their actions. Most of the men there were African-American, so this prison gave you the impression you were back in slavery!

Most of the guys on the tier were incarcerated for more than 20 years. Peanut and Coolie were two men who been incarcerated for more than 30 years. I acquainted myself with them through living on the same tier. Through learning them, I came to knowledge of their stories, pain, and loneliness. I immediately became empathic towards them. I became frustrated and resentful towards the system. That included everyone who created the situation to be this way for these men. God used the situation and these men's stories to teach me about myself as well as about the gifts that dwelled within me.

God allowed me to meet this guy named, "Kevin". Amazingly, Kevin was the first person I met while on lockdown. What a coincidence, this guy held the same name as me. He was on lockdown, on the same tier as me living just 2 cells away from me. He was on lockdown by choice, because he wanted to be away from the madness that came with living around so many people in Angola. Kevin was convicted for "allegedly" executing four (4) white people in an all-white parish. The court sentenced him to four life sentences, one for each count. However, when you met Kevin, you couldn't tell by interacting with him that he held such a barbaric sentence. Kevin was humble, respectable, approachable, and held an organic charisma that was magnetic. He possessed a lot of wisdom and knowledge. I loved his style the moment I met him. He always made you feel comfortable when you were around him.

I learned he knew how to rap. Interestingly, he did gospel rap. One day as he unleashed his rhymes on me, he inquired if I knew how to rap. I told him, "No". I loved rap music, but the thought of myself rapping never crossed my mind. Not only did he know how to rap, but prior to his incarceration he released a rap album. He told me this was his career before he came to prison. Every time I passed his cell I would observe him spending a lot of time writing rap songs. He was compiling and organizing them into albums for the future. He would stand in front of the only window in his cell and rap to himself. He did this with the intentions that upon his release from prison he could easily record his music. I must admit, this fascinated me. Here was a guy sentenced to four (4) life sentences still preparing himself for his future.

Now, I always wanted to learn how to rap, but didn't know how to gracefully compute my words together in a way that what I said rhymed and discharged a flow. Well, I confess, Kevin inspired me to start writing rap music and poetry. He taught me how to format and write it on paper. Kevin told me how and why I should do it. He gave me a logical reason why I should write what I feel and what I had been through on paper. He said, "You never know when you're going to be released from prison. So, telling your story is very important because it educates people about what you went through. What better way to tell your story than through music?" His reasoning made sense. As a result, I started writing rap lyrics and poetry. I wanted other people to hear my voice, see my feelings, and view my life through reading or hearing my rap lyrics. I wrote my first rap song. When it was time to perform in front of Kevin, the one-man audience, I felt nervous for some reason. I couldn't catch up with the beat. We created beats from beating on our chest in a rhythmic manner. However, as I'm rapping the rhymes it felt like they didn't rhyme. I tried to produce a matching beat for the song I created, but this first performance turned into a disaster. Kevin told me to keep writing and practice every chance I get. So, I did. Eventually, I became better and started feeling more comfortable doing it. This was a chance for me to tell my story through the bleeding of ink. I kept writing and before you knew it I had notebooks full of rhymes. Later, when I met my cousin in the parish jail, he taught me how to stay on beat and the importance of inserting my written music into my memory. He knew tidbits on the art because he had a short lived rap career. He said, "When it's in your memory, you could recite it how you wanted to when it came time to perform it." This was wise advice.

In the process of time I was transferred to another prison –Rayburn Correctional Center. I met another guy upon transferring. He recognized the gift before I knew it was a gift. He allowed me to perform my rap songs as poetry, in the form of Spoken Word. He wanted me to do it that way. This guy gave me the opportunity and platform to share my gift with others. I mean other incarcerated men.

This book came into being for the purpose of sharing my gift with others. What good is a gift, skill, or talent if you don't share it with others? The purpose for having the gift, skill, or talent is to share it with someone else who needs it more than you. This gift, skill, or talent you have may be anything, but what good is it, if you don't serve people with it?

I desire to share my gift of writing poetry with the world. I pray that it inspires everyone who reads it. This book is more than poetry, it is my rawest emotions and truest sentiments dispensed in a poetic format.

There is more to come from me, so stay in tune for my next project, *"Black Thoughts: The Angry Black Kid from Reserve Projects"*. This will be a book that offers hope and optimism, inspiring many kids in my generation to be conscious of where you come from and aware of where you plan to go in life.

I offer my heart, mind and soul in *Black Thoughts: Emancipating Kevin X*. I pray this book encourages, inspires, edifies and enlightens someone's spirit that God can do anything, reach anyone and love anyone, no matter who you are or where you may be at in life. God loves you unconditionally, and I pray that He blesses all readers of this book who dare to embark upon this journey with me.

"Lord, I Need Your Help"

Lord I need your help because I can't help myself
I want to do right but Lord I can't fake it
I have desires to do wrong because Lord it's in my nature

Stanza (1)

Sometimes my pride won't let me cry for help, even if my house on fire
I'm too ashamed to ask
I'm caught up in this web of sin,
Sometimes I feel, I'm too guilty to pray,
The right I want to do, I can't,
The wrong I hate, I repeat again.
In sin, did my mother conceive me
The root of this problem goes back to the Garden of Eden
I wonder why, my spirit dead to my Father in Heaven.
Some questions lurk in my soul, that's why I be stressing,
Is it evil forces that really comes against me?
That's why I keep losing this battle?
Damn, it's a hassle in the morning when I wake up,
The wrong I just hate it,
I can't fake it
I'm just insane, these same acts get repeated on a daily basis,
I don't need to go to a mental institution, such as Jackson
Because I'm crazy
My heart needs an operation, and sin is like a cancer
Yea, Christ is the only answer
I need a spirit transfusion just to get better.

I need a Doctor who could heal me where I'm damage
I'm addicted to trapping and lusting after women
I was hook on crime like a junky need that feeling
I'm tired of reaching for the drugs to cover up the shame,
now I'm reaching for that love to cover up my shame
Lord, rescue me from the man, that I see in the mirror
I need another body, because by myself, I can't cure it

Intermission
Lord I need your help because I can't help myself
I want to do right but Lord I can't fake it
I have desires to do wrong because Lord it's in my nature

Stanza (2)

I'm my best friend and my worst enemy
I'm struggling with this sin problem,
It's hard to find victory
Lord, I need your strength more than the food I eat
Please show me the secret to your power,
Please reveal the recipe.
Because I'm calling 911 on this body, because it doesn't like to cooperate
Arrest my eyes for first degree lust,
My mind uses them to fornicate
My words a deadly weapon,
My lips could sink a battleship
Evil thoughts, I wrestle with.
I'm a dead Lazarus, clothed with death itself

I'm the walking dead, without hope,
I don't have no life
I was born just to face His Wrath
My sentence already given if I don't meet the Christ
Judge, please grant me a pardon so I don't have to pay the price
Your Word is what brings me light, Your Word is what sets me free
You granted my appeal before I wrote a writ
You offered your grace so I could conquer sin
You walk out that grave just to live within

Intermission
Lord I need your help because I can't help myself
I want to do right but Lord I can't fake it
I have desires to do wrong because Lord it's in my nature

Stanza (3)

I had no home but this world, no guardian but Satan,
No future but Hell
If I was left in that condition,
I wouldn't live to tell
God is the only Author
He wrote my Story as He will
He killed my flesh on the cross as He took the pain of the nails
A God becoming a Man
To save a child that He loves
My righteous acts like filthy rags in Your sight from above
My best works are stained with fraud motives

And imperfect performance
God, you chose me for this moment
Forgive me of my guilt, cleanse me from my filth
I'm tempted to smoke the Kool when I'm itching for a lift
Religion was a tool but it never gave me strength
Legalism had me fool and it only make me drift back into sin
I was in bondage to a list,
Instructing me how to achieve holiness

"One Mistake"

One mistake cost me all I got
And that's all it takes
One wrong mistake gets you judged by twelve or carried by six
That's what you should expect when you living in the streets

Stanza (1)

It takes a second to get in trouble but it takes a minute to get out
That's what my parents said
I wouldn't listen
I never thought, pulling the trigger would force you to pay attention
Carrying that pistol
Have a lot of consequences, man, open your eyes
I learn it from experience
I'm trying to take this message to the youth
But youngsters got choppers, they won't hesitate to shoot.
We in need of change,
But it's hard because of ignorance, black youths blind to the truth
We need to change! Now! We need a new start
But, it's hard because of rappers promoting to
be a gangster than be who you are
Placing killers as our idols, being real is our title
Imitating people who don't care about us
It's not easy to change I'm not going to sell you no lie
I refuse to hide behind the mask and be in disguise
I been shot at, then shot back, made decisions, got me locked up
Listen, once that bullet leave that pistol then that bullet hit the victim

Live fast, die young only message that you sending-
Don't cry! The police come, say you never meant to do it
You opened the door for the system and their
main goal is trying to lose you

Intermission

One mistake cost me all I got

And that's all it takes

One wrong mistake gets you judged by twelve or carried by six

That's what you should expect when you living in the streets

Stanza (2)

Shout out to the dudes with a life sentence over their head,
Wishing they could go back in the past and fix what they did,
but it's done man, guilt slapping them in the face saying,
"They never will be free from all of the mistakes that they made"
I carry an emotional burden
I'm carrying this load, while traveling this road,
It's crazy, when I tell the homies what I been through,
But, they laugh at me, they tantalize me
My message goes in one ear and out the other
Thus far, I gave them the warning, if they don't change
They headed for destruction!
They don't care what I said, they NOT concerned where I been at
They don't believe in a better path than the street life
Facts!
I know many people in prison, with 4 zeros on a rap sheet, X out of society

Young Brother!
One false move get you penalized so analyze that situation,
Before you go get that pistol
For that dude who tripping, mugging or talking about that killing
I need you to think before you do
Pow! What happened! I never would have imagined,
Gripping that lemon squeeze would turn my day so terrible
So I'm sitting in a prison cell, awaiting to go to court
The victim told my family He not going to show
However, He was the first to take the stand and send me up the road
The state offers me 25, I refused, that's my issue
The DA said, "We going forward with this case
to find him guilty, seriously dude!"

Intermission
One mistake cost me all I got
And that's all it takes
One wrong mistake gets you judged by twelve or carried by six
That's what you should expect when you living in the streets

Stanza (3)

A decision from yesterday, started from a thought
I wrestle with regret now, because I got caught by the law
But Jesus turned it around and changed the way I saw
I sought the truth and learn, I was naive to the lies I believe
Now, my life different than it was before
From stealing out of stores to breaking into houses

To hustling on the corner to taking others money
I robbed people and showed no mercy, then without notice
Your mind elevates to murder.
Facing jail time or shot up facing death
I tend to ask God for another chance
But it was my mistakes that got me here
I had dreams of this dude that made me scared
The dude kept popping in my nightmares,
Telling me;
"You turn my birthday into my worst day!"
"You got me leaving in a hearse early!"
"My picture on a shirt while my family tend the funeral service!"
Tears started to run down my eyes
The trauma I hold inside,
The burdens I carry around deep inside; this
dream is tattooed in my memory
7-18 play across my mind like it's on a TV screen
I want to be me
But the street life turns you out, mold me into clay
Into something I never meant to be
I just want to be free but the street life holds you down

"Wake Me Up"

Lord wake me up from this nightmare I'm living
I see so much evil so I'm forced to keep killing
I'm filled with these demons my finger itching on the trigger

Stanza (1)

I did so much evil in my lifetime
I started stealing candy out of stores when I was eight years old,
Taking money out of my mama purse,
I flight on the block all night, so I brought my rocks to church!
I go home after the service, I lite a Kool and blunt of purp,
Denying the Holy Spirit's work, I received a killer curse.
Homie got murk in front me
His blood covers his body
I attend his funeral, everybody
Screaming and hollering
I walk up to his mama, and say, "I'm sorry for your lost"
No words to comfort her, so I felt like it was my fault
The devil kidnapped my thoughts and rape my dreams.
I listen to this evil pimp, who taught me plots and
schemes, of how to ghost with the 45 XD
He told me,
"Lurk on your prey every day, then you'll give a
soul wings so they could fly out of space"
I listened, so I took pride how I creep, when I eat beef in
the streets I'm not lying to you, this is how I feast.

An enemy get treated, they feel the energy of metal, a
hearse gives him a ride, so they fly to heaven.
Mac-11 on my side, demon in each bullet
Picking the body where they going to abide where they reside forever
Change is better but nothing changes but the weather.

Intermission

Lord wake me up from this nightmare I'm living

I see so much evil so I'm forced to keep killing

I'm filled with these demons my finger itching on the trigger

"I'm Addicted"

Stanza (1)

I'm in denial but I'm addicted
My affections are fixed, my love is mixed with infatuation for
the something I know not good for my soul, but it's true
God you said,
"Kevin, Sacrifice on the alter the thing you bond to; the lady you
cherish most, the person you allowed to bond to your soul"
I said, "But God, our fornication in another dimension, our
chemical imbalance, allows me to provide her sexual provisions."
He said, "Son, this girl will destroy your soul, if
you keep submitting to this position."
God gave me wisdom for my condition.
He gave me a warning and told me what I was risking.
"Son, this the contra-conceptive thought keeping you in imprisoned"
This a warning sign, my early prevention, I see the
warning signals, even though my will is cripple
I told myself, "I can prevent this, I can't prevent this!"
My frail strength allows me to live in the slums
Where I'm enslaved to feeling good, which is my blemish.
I admit, I have a blurry vision when it comes to holy living.
But I want to do right, but these feelings cause me to have feelings
of withdrawal which extends my pain, it leaves me sicken
Now I cried to my Father
The temptations grew stronger
My lust resurrected, as I gave it to my Father
I quit it I am not messing with her, I whispered
to the angel on my shoulder.

Next thing you know I popped the X, I'm rolling, puff
the purple stogie, I start to miss her and notice
I need to be one with my destroyer because it
gives me pleasure for the moment
I feel loaded when I'm with her like when I drink codeine which
have me in slow motion. She like drugs, she my kryptonite.
She like ecstatic feeling I receive from smoking purple weed
I'm superman when I'm sober, but I'm weak for
her. I admit it, I'm addicted to her.

"Where Do People Go When They Die?"

Dudes killed my homie, a real homie
Now he gone forever
Now I ask this question, is he gone live up in hell or heaven?

Stanza (1)

Where do people go when they die?
Yes, I know!
A bullet hit their chest, they take their last breath, then let their soul go.
Mama drop the tears when she told
She prays to the Lord that He will have mercy on their soul
But the path that her son chose, and based on the life that he live
You will one day stand in front of God for the sins that you did
And one day Jesus will replay the movie of your past, you going to regret
You rejected Jesus, for the approval of your friends
Now you laying in front of a reverend but you breathless
Your family crying, want to take the casket with them
They will write the obituary and paint you like an angel
Ignore the fact, you lived life as a gangster,
This is the tell of the street dude who lived his life without thinking
Where do people go when they die?
Heaven or Hell
The spell from the devil keeps us blind
Some men die without ever committing their life to Christ
Consequently, destined for hell
We kill and get killed
Karma come back on you

Never forget death yelling "Revenge!"
One in front of the gun
His blood will be crying for your sins, the universe seeks justice
Screaming and expecting you to die in the Pen
But you refuse to make that choice
Dying in your sin will cost you
One day we all will die, if you take a life
The sentence you deserve is death, lethal injection
Condemned to live in hell
Sometimes time run out, it seems like a spell
You die in the streets without asking God to forgive you
Once you gone, you ask the question, if you going to hell or heaven

---

Intermission
Dudes killed my homie, a real homie
Now he gone forever
Now I ask this question, is he gone live up in hell or heaven?

Stanza (2)

Voice of my brother's blood crying to the Lord from the ground
So much murder in St. John Parish, we can call it "Murder-Town"
I never seen nothing like it
We worship the pistol like an idol
Youngsters preaching violence as the gospel
To them, this good news
No thinking, they pull the trigger as the first move
No love in the streets, babies die from the bullet wounds

Many mothers cry, who?? And it's true
We married the street life as the good wife
She fooled and lured us, as we take the devil's bait just like the fish bite
I was just josing with Kentrell in the old jail
Me and him got tight
But, when he went home
He had to pay for his sins
One day, I learned he laid lifeless in a ditch from
a bullet wound to the head, all night
Me and him was just talking
Playing spades in the cell, But I thought how life is short
It hit me! I can't feel played
K.T. smoked my Homie Turner bad
Casual sent the hit, he a rat
So, K.T. did that bad
He did Turner wrong
Everybody cried, the entire hood was sad and hollered, WHY??
To Lionel
Youngster and Kerriyon got smashed, which was sad
I wonder to myself, where did these people go when they die
In 2013, we drop a lot of tears for the soldiers that died on the field
Herb got killed, then Dee Dee and David got smashed
Too much going on in St. John Parish
I just pray, y'all made it to that place
Where Jesus' Blood wash all your sins
All the soldiers who lost their life
I guess killing each other is a trend
But no one asks the question where do people go when they die

"The Path to Redemption"

Stanza (1)

We Came a Long Way but We Not There Yet
This Path I want to take everybody down
Will educate and shine the light on the dark mind of ignorance
This knowledge is not meant to offend but to encourage and uplift
That we may gain the true knowledge and
destroy the simple mind of ignorance
We Came a Long Way but We Not There Yet
African Americans came a long way from
being labeled property to citizens
1856 Dred Scott decision declared Africans ineligible for citizenship
We Came a Long Way but We Not There Yet
Abraham Lincoln's Emancipation Proclamation
of 1863, declared former slaves free
In 1865, Southern States didn't have State government
Louisiana welcomed the unaccepted reality of emancipation
Legislatures passed black codes to define new legal status
We Came a Long Way but We Not There Yet
This knowledge is not meant to offend but to encourage and uplift
That we may gain the true knowledge and
destroy the simple mind of ignorance

We Came a Long Way but We Not There Yet
The 13th Amendment declaring us free at the same time we paying a fee
The South was Reconstructing the government in 1898
The Louisiana Constitutional Convention Constructed
The Criminal Justice Judicial System

Saying 9 jurors were enough to convict a citizen
We Came a Long Way but We Not There Yet
Non-unanimous verdicts were legal during the Jim Crow Era
But the 14th Amendment gave us citizenship fully incorporating
The 6th Amendment which guaranteed of a unanimous verdict
But were we worthless? Were we not considered a citizen in the first place?
We Came a Long Way but We Not There Yet
An article stated, "White supremacy was the intent of non-unanimous verdicts against African Americans".
I'm not racist, but this crazy, because we supposed
to be celebrating African History
We Came a Long Way but We Not There Yet
In 1972, the U.S. Supreme Court ruled in Apodaca v. Oregon which
endorsed the use of split jury verdicts in Louisiana and Oregon
Were African Americans a target?
We Came a Long Way but We Not There Yet
MLK said He had a dream we wouldn't be judged by the
color of our skin but the content of our character
We Came a Long Way but We Not There Yet
In 2019, Louisiana voted for change, passing an
amendment requiring unanimity in jury verdicts
We Came a Long Way but We Not There Yet
The U.S. Supreme Court granted certiorari in Ramos v. Louisiana
We Came a Long Way but We Not There Yet
120-year practice may face its day
We await to bring justice to the African-American race
But, why did the United States Supreme Court deny
retroactive application of *Ramos* in *Edwards v. Vannoy*?

They said it would put a burden on the state to grant new trials
to every person convicted by non-unanimous jury verdicts
Hold up! This a law from the Jim Crow era that is still lurking?
It sounds like they stand by the racist rhetoric from the past
The racist mentality that still stands, the clan
traded in their white sheets for black robes

We Came a Long Way but We Not There Yet

The path to redemption is a hard path to take, making society a better
place, is not the case, equality and freedom to the African-American race
I thought we were there, but we come a long way, I think white
supremacy is trying to take back their rightful place
The powers that be said it's up to the Louisiana Supreme Court to make
it right and grant new trials to people convicted by a Jim Crow law
What they did was despicable and hateful, denying retroactive
application of Louisiana v. Ramos in the Reddick case
This the racist state, that agrees with upholding
Jim Crow laws and allowing them to stay
Who will set us free?
Thanks to the Greats who paved the way, white or black, slave or free
Thank the Creator for Grace, because we need
His strength traveling along the way
Because we going backwards instead of going ahead
rectifying all wrongs committed against a race
Who suffered in slavery and still not free till this day
Abraham Lincoln's Decree only pissed racists off, causing
them to demonstrate bigotry and prejudice to me
Justice without mercy is no justice at all

We Came a Long Way but We Not There Yet

"Lord, I'm Undefeated"

Stanza (1)

I'm Undefeated,

I believe it

The blood stronger than demons

What Jesus did at the cross

Is the power to save the lost

Help me pick up your word for the day of battle

I feel like I'm curse

As I walk upon this earth

Yahshua bear my sins that's what Jesus said

That I'll go free

And Jesus be judged for the entire human race

Only believe in his blood that could rescue you

This evil nature entraps me to money, murder, and women

Since Adam took a bite of this apple

I'm forever affected

The price I owed God

I could never repay

When His Justice is the District Attorney

His mercy is my attorney

Defending me always

Pleading my case

When I stand in front of the judge

I feel so guilty

A man stood up in court

I never seen before

He said,

"Can you release him? I want to take the lick! I want to pay
the penalty that Kevin really deserves, let me be punished
for the crime or offense Kevin really deserves!"
This really struck a nerve in me
I thought to myself,
"What type of man would get some nails drove through His hands?"
I stood there amazed, feeling loved
He took a chance on me
I know I was a mess
If Jesus didn't take the charge, I could never save myself

Stanza (2)

A slave feeling defeated in bondage use to this treatment
Lord, I'm dealing with some problems
I have to be honest
It came from evil desires
I can't do right
But, I keep trying
I noticed my flesh singing to do wrong like a gospel choir
I ask God
Take me higher
Take me there
Where you at where it's pure
I'm so polluted
Woe is me
Your presence me want to flee
Your holiness I cannot see
I'm controlled by these demons
They using me to do evil

I'm longer for a healer
I'm soul screaming for Jesus
My spirit feel defeated
My mind is just confusion
Yahshua come to my rescue
I'm drowning come be my come be a lifeguard
In danger come be my refuge
We committed regicide, I'm the one who killed my king
Blood squirt from His hands
The chastisement of our peace
He was despised and rejected of men
Romans nailed Him to a tree
His precious blood drip
Because of my murder and pride
Jesus was spit on and humiliated
So I could be justified sat on high
He never stops loving us
No matter how far we run
His mercy doesn't care what we done

"In the Prison of Unforgiveness"

Stanza (1)

I'm confined behind these walls
Some view me as a horse, trapped in a stall
Being vigilant, expecting to be release,
Please, check my vital signs, my vigor growing weak
Time keep going, I'm anxious to be free,
In bondage to fear
Of what one would do to me,
Tears are frosted flakes, because revenge is all I seek
Its hate that I only drink
I get 3 chows a day
Bitterness, Resentment, and Unforgiveness
I feed my soul poison, as I transform into a victim of self-pity
In the prison of unforgiveness
I'm taking ibuprofen to cure my sickness
Vivacious feelings of retaliation I envision,
I listen to the voice of resentment, seeing my enemies' dead
No longer living, I crave healing.
But, I'm addicted to the pain of holding unforgiveness in my system
Forgiveness means not harboring angry feelings against those who harm us
My consciousness keeps telling me, "Lay down the right to get even".
An unforgiving spirit binds us to the evil leader, Satan, who
governs those that won't forgive people who hurt them
My anger not directed at the person who hurt
me, but aimed at others in my path
So much time passed, I thought I forgiven them for what they did.
Pictures of what they did to me, I see, remind me it wasn't fair

They off the hook?
But, look at the damage that's been done,
Word to the wise,
"Unforgiveness" prevents you from worshipping God,
It blocks my view of his perfect love
The very love He longs for me to have
The nature of unforgiveness begins with a declaration,
"I refuse to give to others, what God has given so freely to me".
You have to suffer to understand forgiveness,
in order to forgive, you must suffer
Word to the wise,
Pray to God and ask Him to release you from
the chains that incarcerate your soul,
I ask You, Father, to release me from the prison of unforgiveness.

"I wish"

Stanza (1)

I wish I could fly in the clouds, live in Heaven, chill with God
while I feel His Presence
Where there is:
No more, evil; no more, stressing.
No more, murder; No more, pressure;
To do wrong because I'm in His presence
Only defeated demons, and a defeated Devil
Imagine streets of gold, where I reside forever
Me and Christ live together, I will possess a special body
That's made to live forever
Having Christ, is my biggest treasure
The greats mastered the body while the greatest mastered the mind
I wish I could rewind time, and bring my mother back
Feel the pain she felt inject me with the virus that
killed her and experience her death
This a silent cry I had, I wish I could hold your hand again
Tell her, "I love you",
Just to see your smile again
To tell her "I'm sorry" for the pain I cause
her and the decisions that I made
I wish I could speak with you just one more time
Tell you how I changed and grown into a
great man, as a result of your mind
You gave me wisdom, knowledge and understanding
I promise to honor your legacy and take care of family

"Don't Put More on Me Than I Can Bear"

Stanza (1)

Nights in a cell, I felt neglected
My family didn't answer the phone when I fell,
I felt rejected
My family was by themselves, un-protected
My son without his father, feeling neglected
My friends let me down, it was expected
My friends were reckless, so I had to dissect them
My girlfriend lied and did me wrong, she was reckless
I can't trust to many people, so the pistol on the dresser
When I go to sleep, I feel peace
I kept a burner for dudes, who wanted to test me
But it's so much pressure, when you in live a desert, with
snakes, vipers, and rats who want to entrap you
I went to trial, ignorant of the law,
The system desires to take my life
Because I'm young, black and blind to my rights
Crystal clear I'm the victim, when you have a deficient mind in the fight
Industrial Complex System eat black boys for dinner
You really an innocent victim in the fight
I was blind, deaf and numb, demise was my plight
They punish me for being black and ignored my rights
The gift, the constitution afforded me was never given,
I thought I get a jury of my peers, but I received an all-white jury,
who wasn't pure, they convicted me without the evidence
Three said I was not guilty, and didn't commit the
crime, nine said I did it and should serve time

But the judge sent them, to reevaluate the evidence
Nine not enough to convict me in the State of Louisiana
One man changed his vote at the last minute,
Once the judge coerced him to do it
Is it legal to be coerced? Threaten and influenced by judicial officials
Who instructed to honor the constitutions' jurisprudence?
I was convicted by a 10-2 jury verdict, an illegal
verdict that is traced to white supremacy
Non-unanimous jury verdicts rooted in Jim Crow and racism
The reason for making the law was to establish the white man's hate for me
They wanted to establish white supremacy and
Disenfranchise African-Americans in the jury process
How far they will go, just to show, we animals and beasts who
don't deserve due process that the constitution affords
Lord, don't put more on me than I can bear
I suffered the blow of the racists' hand when I was convicted by an all-white criminal justice system, who adores re-enslaving young black boys
Sending me to Angola to reside, contributing to black genocide
Black men make up 33 percent of the State of Louisiana's population
Why does 67 percent remain incarcerated?
Lord, save me and my people
From a system broken and in need of freedom
Lord, don't put more on me than I can bear

"I Feel Like a Ghost"

I feel like a Ghost sometimes buried alive
Locked up in a place sentenced to die
Estranged from my love ones
Is killing me inside
I feel like a Ghost sometimes to the people I use to live with
To the world I use to live in

Stanza (1)

Talk on the phone and at the visits,
I'm the friendly Casper
I disappeared from their thoughts as soon as I hang up
It's like I vanished
It was magic, the way I vanished, from the world,
But this is what I get
From living life as a savage, my right thumb was
sleeping on the hammer of the 45
I was itching for a kill as a youngster, I should have gone the other way
But I saw him, gunned down in front me
Now, I'm sentenced to 20 flat
I'm just another story to my homies
If I would have known what I know now
I'll be home on my knees, asking the Lord to help me live right.
I watch myself get buried alive, my mom attended the funeral of my trial
The jury said "Your guilty!". The judge sentences me to die
The judge sends me to Angola
And tried to take what I love,

Angola lock me down for no reason
For mail call, I don't hear my name
I feel distant from my people;
I raise a boy, raised him until he was one year's old
I thought I was the father, later I learn, that's not my son
My girlfriend played mind games and brought him to
visit me and said tell your daddy, "You love him"
Tyree stared in my eyes like he looking at a ghost
She put the phone to his ear and told Tyree again,
"Tell your daddy you love him",
It's hurting me inside but I wear the coat of a father
I just feel like a ghost

Intermission
I feel like a Ghost sometimes buried alive
Locked up in a place sentence to die
Estranged from my love ones
Is killing me inside
I feel like a Ghost sometimes to the people I use to live with
To the world I use to live in

Stanza (2)

When you out of sight and out of mind
Believe me, nobody thinking of you, when you josing, doing time
Not too many people sent me money, not too many wrote a letter
But Dee was my only homeboy who came seen me on a visit

I could count on my hand who put money on Securus
So, sometimes I was tripping
How could people say one thing, then do something different
Disappointment left me bitter, my momma said on the phone,
"Son, It's going to be better in the future".
But, I got angry as I listened, stressing when looking at a picture
I hated that I'm invisible to the ones I want to see me,
I write people letters I get no answer,
Call their phones they disconnected it
Yes, I get the message, I'm dead in their world,
No life went on hold
When I was arrested, but my mother kept it real
My son, Tyree has another daddy but I can't trip on Jarcelle
Tyree even though you're not my son, I love you!!
I miss you, and would never forget you
Even though I'm in prison, just know it hurts, because I'm in here
It hurts because I can't be there
I feel like a Ghost while I'm in here

"See the World Through My Eyes"

Take a look through my eyes, see what I see
No love in these souls
Take a look through my eyes, see what I see
Where hearts turn cold

Stanza (1)

Look at the bigger picture! Looking at the world
through my third eye, you could see it clearer
I see my reflection in the mirror
I see a great man, but society see a killer
They don't understand justice is blind
How could they judge me, when they have a log in their eye
My lawyer keeps telling me, "Take the deal" …
"Kevin, please settle!"
When I signed that contract for that plea
That deal I made with the state
It felt like I sold out to the devil
You believe I had two lawyers on my case
Saying, "Kevin you will not win this battle!"
I told them lawyers, really it doesn't matter,
I really rather, shake the dice and take the gamble
And allow twelve people decide the matter
I can't admit to a crime I didn't commit, just
admit to squeezing that hammer
I had fear in my emotions; this was special pressure just for me
Lawyers coercing me to accept the plea

Using fear in that moment to get me to agree
Black boys always felt that way since slavery
It was meant for me to be scared
Never trust a white man in a suit
See the world through my eyes,
Let me give you this lecture of this place I call "Time"
In this place, stress eat your hair away
Dudes go bald in their prime
This a place where some been there for a dime
Some been there for twenty-five
Some have forty years' in
Man, it makes me cry, some go crazy in this place
Some have no escape, sad reality they will die in this place
They are the walking dead in the Pen
A lot of my friends' blind on the outside
They killing committing crimes
Like the streets don't have a fine
Man, when you all in, it causes you to chase death
Go to the Pen and do time, get entrapped
After that, you see it all
I see men turn into fags
They were head busters on the streets,
Now, they sit on toilets when they piss
This made me sick, made me gag
Once upon a time, these dudes impersonated a gangster,
Man, these ~~niggers~~ trick,
Some hustle to pay the lawyer
Plugging drugs in their ~~ass~~ through visits, make their family take the risk

Have to do it to survive, do it by any means
Some hustle just for approval by others, just to be seen

Intermission
Take a look through my eyes, see what I see
No love in these souls
Take a look through my eyes, see what I see
Where hearts turn cold

Stanza (2)

The picture I want to paint, because you can't look in my eyes
And see my pain
Living in prison made me sick with shame,
I was unaware of its entrance, made me blame
Everyone who caused me pain
In prison I couldn't sleep
I was oppressed by depression
Like I caught a plane on my way
Flying to the island of the mental insane
In a place without your family and friends
I'm emotionally drained
It's been more than 3,000 days in this prison asylum
I was a 17-year-old boy when I left and got in that car
And took that ride with that boy, experience this trauma
The process to be a slave is long and awful
I go to court looking like the villain

I had to wear red clothes to represent a killer, as I attended court
The media already painted the picture that I killed him
You innocent until proven guilty
I was housed with my peers, young boys just like me,
Nothing change, just like the slaves back then,
Awaiting to be auctioned off
To the nearest slave-owner disguised as a DOC Warden
Black Boys been getting snatched by the Department of Corrections
Been getting cornered off, I resent my environment
My vision not clear, what's my next move
Dudes been in Angola so long, fear have you thinking,
what it takes for me not to be in their shoes
Thoughts of anxiety and worry infuse my mind
I wanted to cry, what should I do
I kept thinking about one decision costed me to wear these shoes
I feel like I'm curse
A verdict killed my dreams and caused my hope to ride in a hearse
I wanted to die and leave this earth
All the people that I hurt
I finally reaped what I sow
I have a lot of pain and trauma tattooed on my soul
Asking God, "Why Me? Why Me, Lord?"
I know wasn't perfect, I feel less than a human
being, less than a person without a purpose

Intermission
Take a look through my eyes, see what I see
No love in these souls

Take a look through my eyes, see what I see
Where hearts turn cold

Stanza (3)

What do you see when you look in my eyes?
Love or Hate?
In my world, could you relate?
Where you see no door of escape
Trapped for 40 years in a place
As I was taking a ride in the police car,
I realize I'm a slave again, trapped behind bars
Going to court once a week, standing in the courtroom where you can't speak your peace
White judge, white lawyer and white DA
Holding court, discussing how long can this slave do, only if he takes a plea
I can't cry, they tell me, "Shut up!" …
"Don't Speak!"
Lulled into a misapprehension of the state's case
The white District Attorney ("DA") said, "Should he get 10 to 40 or a Life Sentence?"
He was a juvenile based on Miller v. Alabama
In 35 years, we could grant him a hearing
"Hell No!", the white lawyer said acting like he defends me
It was a code to get me 35 years.
I have 35 fears, could I explain and tell you my side of the story
"No!"
You a killer without hope

He sent me to Angola where I been around dudes
who really had cancer, on the brink of death
I talked with Uncle Rick before He died, Doctor
dropped the ball, not telling Rick, he was sick
I prayed with him, hours before he took his last breath
On the tier when John committed suicide
Really made me think, really made me cry
("Department of Corrections") D.O.C have Doctors who
offenders and convicted felons, and it's not a crime?
Taking care of patients, but their help not worth a dime
Take a look through my eyes

"On My Back"

I have the world, the devil and flesh on my back
The victim's family coming to court want me sentenced to death
It's messed up because the life I lived
They don't care about my freedom they want me to die in the pen

Stanza (1)

I'm living in, enemy occupied territory
My energy spent living, this atrocious evil story
My flesh wants to win and it wants the glory
Let me introduce you to my friend, pride,
Yes, it's my trophy
I was arrested by a spell from this world, the
prince of this world have my focus
I detested the trail you leave, when you take a man soul
Seeing his family fiend for revenge, their hearts turn cold
They dreaming his killer bleed, you watch hatred transform their soul
And they truly believe, you get justice, from a justice system
Where a jury member knows the victim's family members and
They pay him to vote you guilty
Based on, how the victim's family feeling
Where is the justice?
Then they want the judge to sentence you to
death and die old in the penitentiary
It's cold, because it's no forgiveness
I feel claustrophobic in my soul; they clog my freedom in the system
I sneezed, its cold, mucus! It leaves me sickening

I walk in the courtroom, in a red jumpsuit
My rap sheet paper is blue so society say I'm finished
Demarcation, separated from my nation.
Face the judge, array my name, to them, I'm nothing but a slave;
A decoration in chains.

Intermission
I have the world, the devil and flesh on my back
The victim's family coming to court want me sentenced to death
It's messed up because the life I lived
They don't care about my freedom they want me to die in the pen

---

Stanza (2)

Sometimes I wish and imagine, I could stand in front of the judge
And say, "Your Honor, my flesh shot him!"
I bet, I'll walk on the murder
And get out the same hour, I'll look at the DA and smirk
Watch the victim's relatives get angry, tell me I'm a coward
But that's if we lived in an imaginary world
His mama wants me dead
Because someone murk her son, I can't replace him
They want me dead on a shirt, the devil continually rides my back
He wants to destroy me and want to kill me
Then he passes me the strap so I purchased his curse
My mind a mess listening to this devil and his crap
His ally is my flesh when you take a soul it's no turning back
Young dudes killing for no reason

Some get convicted for murder, die in Angola
Some come home and let their closest friend smoke them
My friend got proved wrong, let his closest homie cut throat him
Put the chrome to his dome and told him you have to go because I owe you
His last words before he shoots, "I took the hit!"
I'm Judas killing you to get rewarded, Fifty-Five Hundred!
The killer never seen all the money, the cops caught him for the murder
He doing time for nothing, ruthless man with a soul, as he murdered

---

Intermission

I have the world, the devil, and flesh on my back

The victim family coming to court want me sentenced to death

Its messed up because the life I live

they don't care about my freedom they want me to die in the pen

---

Stanza (3)

I was praying to the Lord, asking God to change Kevin
Evil thoughts flashed cross my mind, Satan I know it's you!
Yes, it's coming from the devil! I hate I can't think straight
I gave in to the devil's game
So I settle
This guilty feeling, I can't escape so I'm feel pressured
I tried to pray but I got up off my face
This demon just won't let up, when you pray
Demonic spirits fight harder, territory of the spirit
Evil love to cross your border,
Me versus a demon, he has more power

One of them equal a legion, an entire empire
I can't see him, but he sees me, he has the advantage when I'm tired
The devil come in different shapes and forms
When you enslaved to sin
You and the devil in the boxing ring, and he's favored to win
He felt like I took a soul, so it's eye for an eye and tooth for a tooth,
He believes, I could never escape his grip, but he really is fooled
Me and a demon playing chess, we gamble for my soul
I'm thinking of ways to finesse him, to take over his board
Then the demon hollered, "Check!", he tries
to checkmate me with his pawn
Then he tries to flex, acting like I loss
I got no respect for demons, Jesus have my soul!
I got the world, the devil, and flesh on my back
Demons use me as pawns in the streets, got me thinking I'm trap
Having sex with a demon while I'm sleeping
Wake up from dreaming, realize I'm in jail,
Sperm on my pants
Pissed off, angry I waste a fetus, so I took a bird bath in a cell
I hate to displease God like Onan and waste my fetus in my hand
Jesus allowed me to fall in a prison, serving a harsh sentence,
so he could get my soul out of the devil's hand
If Jesus wouldn't have save me
I would be sentenced to hell according to the devil's plan

"Don't Count Me Out"

Don't count me out yea I'll be back
I been gone for a minute but now I'm free at last
Don't count me out because I'll be back

Stanza (1)

I talk about it, I dreamt about it
I envisioned this day, when I got out them gates
No orange, no more chains, no court dates, no more wet dreams
Free at last! From this nightmare if you could walk in my size 10
I was a child charged with murder
The district attorney tried to get me sentenced to 80 years
For crimes I never heard of
I felt so depressed and alone like a ghost, to all my people
I vanished from their thoughts, soon as the phone hang up
This pain started to creep in,
Went to visit through a glass
We talked for 15 minutes, but I became history
They only mentioned me when speaking of the past
"He never would be free again" some of my friends said
They laughed, he's stuck in a cell, haters counted me out, even my family
The time the judge sentenced me to don't even fit on a clock
The white judge gave me numbers I couldn't calculate in my brain
She failed to consider mitigating factors that show
and demonstrate my underdeveloped brain
The DA thought he seen a demon,
But God seen His image, a young man greater than an angel

God seen me in my worst state, restored me to my birth place
He rescued me from Angola, a cursed place
Praise be to God because I plead for His mercy
I prayed to the Lord many nights, He'll let me get out

Intermission

Don't count me out yea I'll be back

I been gone for a minute but now I'm free at last

Don't count me out because I'll be back

"The Pain Won't Go Away"

Stanza (1)

Pain could be described in so many words,
People normally feel pain on different levels
They may feel: affliction, agony, anguish,
distress, misery, torment, or torture
All these different feelings subscribe to someone feeling pain
Which all give a vivid picture of what pain is to them
The picture I want to paint will tell you how pain makes
me and many others in the same position feel,
This pain makes me feel sick with shame
Unaware of its entrance makes me blame, other people or myself
For its uninvited stay, this pain oppresses me
It keeps me in depression,
Makes me feel like I'm going deeper in a trap
Like I'm going off the deep end without family or friends,
This loneliness I feel; I can't pretend it don't hurt
I went to Angola as a child, I felt isolated and by myself for awhile
I'm stamped as a slave, the system finally got me
Stamped me with this DOC number
This the same system my ancestors tried to escape and warn me about
My ancestors died trying to get free
Society hate me, causing me to drown in fear, I resent my environment
My vision not clear, the slave master laughs at my entrapment
I developed hatred for him, in order to survive his capture
And I'm not trying to be his victim but the inevitable happened
My abhorrence of being here, I mutilated my tears
Who will cry for the little boy?

The jailer said, "You deserve to be here!".
My pain won't go away, one decision became an epidemic
Affecting many people at one time
A verdict destroyed my dreams, proclaiming death over
my hope of being free, I cried not for you to see
My pain is tattooed on my soul, I'm traumatized
All of my basic human needs have been undermined
My need to feel safe and have the ability to feel Ok
Has been taken away
I lost the ability to have self-esteem and dream of being free
Being in prison causes me to feel pain
Traumatic Prison Experience is the exchange.
Intimacy with a woman has been taken away
I can't reproduce or produce fruit, what do you want me to do or say?
My ability to have control is taken away, you have to be counted everyday
An autocratic ruler enforcing his rules telling me how,
when, and where to live in this prison place
Prison undermines all of my basic human needs
causing me to feel pain on another level
This torture and affliction causes me to believe this pain, is the devil
It won't go away

I dedicate this next poem to Aubrey Brown, my niece who died at birth and lived a short life. I love you and we will never forget about you baby girl.

"What Would It Be Like if You Were Here"

What would it feel like to hold you in my arms?
What would it be like to see you stand on your own?
What would it feel like to send you off to prom?
What would it be like to see you get married?
What would it be like to walk you down the aisle?
What would it be like if you were here?

Stanza (1)

What would it be like if you were here? a
question I asked myself many times
I'm your uncle who never had the chance to meet you and see you smile
I wish I could hold you for your first birthday
I wondered what it would be like to see you walk for the first time?
Utter your first words, like they were rhymes
To see a child who is silent utter a sound, its magic
You were so precious when death entered on a cold
night and snatched you away from your parents
I felt tears run down my face as I thought about your mother and your
daddy's family, the troubled soul everyone encountered when you died
I was in Angola fighting for my life when Kim birthed you

Kim's heart turned cold when she lost you
Your death rocked our family core structure
People don't understand the pain of a mother when she loses a child
Tears rain down on a mother's soul
Sadness is appropriate when losing a baby is like losing your smile
Now I write this poem
Wondering what it would be like if you were here
Would the pain she felt back then now disappear if you were here
What would it be like if you were here, what comfort a man could give
What understanding he could show her to make her feel comfort
None came, you died before you could experience your first birthday
Before you could meet Kingston and Ray'Lynn
Both of them are sweet and precious children
They your younger siblings, now she feels cursed
Instead of celebrating your birth she had to bury
you and order a shirt with you on it
She had to follow a hearse
What would it be like if you were here
To see you smile and to see what makes you fear or be afraid
This can't be real you disappeared into eternity!
You are in heaven, in Jesus' arms, grown up,
When we see you again
You'll be who you were meant to be, looking
down on Kingston and Ray'Lynn
See your brother and sister grow strong
He looks just like your mother; I wonder what it would be like to see you
Playing with Hara, Rosie, Bunny, Lo, Ron and Kyla, your cousins
Who loves you

I could see you going to church with your grandmother
and she teaching you about Jesus
I see your Paw Paw Kevin giving you that love that last forever
I wonder what it would be like if you were here
Now you have your Grandmother and Aunt Bridgett to keep you company
I know y'all smiling
I love you and miss you
I never will forget you

"You Wasn't There"

You weren't there when I needed you
You didn't care when I needed you
You never helped when I needed you
Now how it feels to walk in my shoes

Stanza (1)

You weren't there, you didn't care
Never shared the moments that I had
Never prepared to hold it down through the thick and thin
I was isolated and separated in the Pen
A team keeps it real, but you sold me, dreams with your pen
You wrote me love letters, you said you had my back
Deep within, you never face the fact- you wasn't built like that
You lied to my face, you never cared how I felt
You said, "No man, would ever take your place"
These were lines you wrote, you thought were the appropriate thing to say
You hid your hand in my venerable state,
You didn't stick to the plan you made
The plan we had, you gave up
You couldn't keep the phone on
So excuses you gave
My visits, were looking at your pictures, staring at the ceiling
I was pissed off, I thought to myself, "I was always there
for you that's why, I'm always in my feelings"
I'm feeling disappointed, because I'm absent from your presence
I was stalking the vision, that I'll return to your presence

But, when we face to face, I'll have a few questions
Did you ever make the efforts? to stick by my side
When I was held captive
Were you ready to ride?
All them nights I was stressing and wanted to cry
I was a friend of depression, and thought I was losing my mind

---

Intermission
You weren't there when I needed you
You didn't care when I needed you
You never help when I needed you
Now how it feels to walk in my shoes

Stanza (2)

I was trapped in a place, charged with a case
Indicted for murder
A witness I face
I learn facing that L
All my ladies walked away
I call my girl from jail, her turn
Games she play
Will you jose me? "Yea", she said
"But Kevin, I got bills to pay"
Every time I ask for something
She moves at her pace, after sentencing day
She slowly fades away, she took the cake
When she built a case

All of sudden, she hates me because I'm locked up in this place
Thinking I'm not coming home
So she leaves me, no trace of her
So she avoids the feeling of me not coming home one day

Stanza (3)

Blame me Blame me, yea I blame myself
My baby mama made statements
Yes! she made a deal, with the victim's family
She sold her child for 5 grand, in exchange
That she testifies against me
Got me going insane, she feeling guilty
When she visits me, we in the visit booth
She dropping tears so she blames me
For everything she going through
I look at her through the glass window before I speak, I listen
If It wasn't for you killing dude, I wouldn't be in this position
How you going to blame me when I'm innocent
of the crime I allegedly committed
She come to visit pregnant,
Telling me that's my baby
She keeps venting and tripping about me being the father
I questioned her motives and figure she was lying
just so she could feel sorry for me
She got the nerve to tell me
You the one I'm stressing over and deeply in love with
She deceived me all this time
It's really the other dudes she misses being with
I fall for her lies

My Momma said, "Son pay attention!"
I failed to listen, I was more loyal to people who constantly showed me no love and un-loyal to those who constantly gave me their all expressed through their love

"My Story"

Stanza (1)

Once upon a time, born a young man
Live on East 14th Street
I was raised by Sarah Jean and Kevin
They did all they could
They tried to raise me as a Christian
Grew up in the hood
With no brothers, just 4 sisters,
Now, across the street was the projects,
And looking from a distance
That life glistened in my eyes, I heard gunshots and seen pistols
Seen drugs sold, seen nice cars
Seen pretty women
The click growing up was; Dee, Nut, Bee and Lil Kenneth
But, this void started to grow
I wanted it all and some more
I craved to be a trap star
Being in the NBA, walked out of my dreams
like it exited out of the back door
I was influenced, and filled my ears with Young Jezzy and Lil Boosie
Next thing I know, the Revolver became my best friend
These thoughts flooded my mind
What would happen if I shoot one?
I quitted school, it was foolish
I smoked Kools on the usual
I tried to puff the pain away
I was seeking for some peace

This is my life, my story, you got to see
Even though it wasn't a good hand
I have to play the hand that was dealt to me

Stanza (2)

Running through Reserve Projects showed me everything:
From stealing to drug dealing to lying to murder
to showing no feelings to women
And, the game was a snake
It bit me with his fangs
The venom hit my system as it ran through my vein
I was addicted to a life, where you trap in a lane
I prayed to the Lord every night, so much wrong I got dull to a right
The streets kept calling my name so it's a fight
Man this so sicken
I'm too guilty to change cause I'm a fourth offender
I started pushing drugs
The money started glistening
Power was a goal, I desired as a position
"Don't go in them bricks", Momma said as she was tripping
But now, I see what she was saying
I thought being a gangster was how you be a man
I was insecure and ashamed
I hurt people, I was the blame
This hurt was rooted in when pops left,
I craved a man's respect, even to the point of death
I had thoughts of suicide, I attempted to commit
I grew up in a godly home
But, my parents wondered where I went wrong

Let me touch someone's heart through this poem
I went to church every Sunday
Mama said, "God loves you" I knew God had a plan
I was naïve and deceived
Being a thug
Took over my dreams
I accepted Christ, now I'm change
I go around old friends, and don't curse
They thinking I'm strange

"Rain On Me"

Stanza (1)

Sometimes, life so painful, it forces you to pray
God allowed me, to break my ankle, so I could depend on Him
I wonder if you were angry with me, why you took my strength?
I ponder the danger I'm in, is it because I sin?
I know the price of change isn't cheap, you pay it when you repent
I feel so guilty and ashamed, so
I'm silent because of sin.
Holy Creator, I was meant to serve you
But I've forsaken your holy truths, I'm afraid, I'm naked,
I been acting like a fool, under Your Wrath don't forsake me
Because I am imperfect, unworthy, and not acting like you!
I was created and raised to be in your shoes
Created in Your Image, meant to conquer evil according to Your Truth;
Evil want to take me, the Devil want to rule,
Satan want to enslave me; He want to keep me glued
He knows what I'm facing, so He use it as his tool
When you blind to the truth you live in a lie
I couldn't recognize the disguise, but I learnt they were wearing masks
Being in disguise, betrayal hurt like a rod, getting stab from behind
I should've listen to the signs,
I got to pay a check for my freedom
I don't have a dime to pay them
They talking about doing time, they call it a fine, that I have to repay
You have to stay enslaved all day confined to the bind that you're in,
All because of;
Mistakes that I made judging me for sin I didn't commit

I'll pay them but when I do, I'm cautious to never repeat the sin
I know one mistake in the streets, could cost your freedom
I was feeling discouraged, so I fell on my knees to pray,
I was thinking about the deal on the table, it was making me scared
The state got a case, so they said
I'm mad, it's not fair,
Me and Renzo said a prayer in the cell,
Knowing they don't care
The District Attorney got numbers over my head like
clouds in the air, these feelings that I'm feeling
You can't comprehend it
Spare me the self-pity I don't want to hear it,
I'm not the victim, nevertheless a victim to the system
Prison sicken, lies that I'm hearing
The devil spitting lies in my ear, got me missing healing
Man, I'm tripping, I pled guilty to manslaughter
Heat of passion, I allegedly did the killing
I falsely confessed
To a crime I never committed,
How many black boys did the same thing out of fear?
How many black boys admitted to being guilty when they were innocence?
My legal situation reminded me,
The constitution never meant for me to be included!
The Louisiana Criminal Procedure meant for me to be excluded,
Am I a Jason or these people really racist?
I don't care, they crazy
I was forced to learn their law
Rain on me, I had to learn how to read and study criminal law
And, know who God is,

But in the system they taught me
How they don't care, separated me from my family and friends
I was guilty before they thought of my innocence
Looking through their lens
It depends what standard measures my sins
They make the alcohol and arrest you for drinking it
Rain on me because I seek revenge
I learn what you don't put behind you, will eventually
define you resulting in confining you
But, I know God prepares you before He propels you into your purpose

Stanza (2)

I face my accuser; the witness takes the stand; the witness
points their finger, that's how they release their anger
But, my 6th Amendment right, guarantee I confront my witness
The streets so vicious I'll send my homies on a mission
I'm so sicken I'll kill my own homies if he snitching
Lord forgive me I'm tired, and finished with the streets
I fell victim to people's opinions
Got to beef with my own kind because they ignorant
They judge me and pass sentence
Hold grudges because I don't listen
Darla told the cops I'm evil and kept a pistol
Same woman I sold weed to and had a son in prison
Lord, don't let them judge me for the same sins they committing
Now, who is the sinner?
But Isolation is devastating to the human soul
Solitary confinement is considered cold
I live through the crudest judgement

A cell eats at your soul
I live through 23 and 1
23 hours in cell alone and one hour on a hall
But I never fold
I'm still rising when I'm done
Still thriving in a grave
I promise to meet the sun
I'm grinding for change

"I Can't Breathe"

Stanza (1)

Breathing and life work together like a doctor and nurse
Breath and life are two intricate elements that make humans live
The breath of life is a gift from God
Our physical bodies function and thrive in the
environment of breathing in air
This parasympathetic side of the body incorporates breathing
in air unconsciously without informing or making us aware

I Can't Breathe

I can't breathe is an utterance not stemming from a lack of oxygen but
from systemic racism that embodies the infrastructure of society
Likewise, the Criminal Justice System heightens its function
off of discriminating and disproportionately treating a
group or class of people differently from one another

I Can't Breathe

Mr. Officer get your foot off my neck
Why do you seem so bold with intimidating me?
Why are you so hostile and agitated based on your first impression of me?
Is it due to the color of my skin?
The way my hair carries this lion like arrogance with a nappy texture
Or is it the dreads in my head that make you afraid?
Or is it the way I walk with this groove of rhythmical notion
that make you feel uncomfortable and insecure?
Or is it your genetic inhabited infrastructure that makes you feel
superior over the minority race, especially African-Americans?
Please get your foot off my neck! I can't breathe!

Discrimination is the new race because you can't call me "Nigger"
no more, you call me "Inmate" and "convicted felon"!

I Can't Breathe

I was free a long time ago when the Emancipation
Proclamation was declared but you didn't care
You wanted segregation and separation
You wanted to legally lynch my people, exile us to
prison and destroy the entire generation
You still want to be the slave master and apex of civilization

I Can't Breathe

You conceived the Jim Crow Era but this era has ended
However, you still practice this segregation through a system
In the educational system

I Can't Breathe

In the HealthCare system

I Can't Breathe

In the Criminal Justice System

I Can't Breathe

But, as my ancestors live and embody this generation awakening
the dead, breathing awareness into my people's ignorant mind
I scream:
"Let there be light, Consciousness Awake!"
I scream get your foot off my neck
I shall arise from this and breathe in the midst of it

I Can't Breathe

George Floyd knew what this meant and I hope their foot loses strength
Oppressing black people is a sin I stand against
At first, I thought that foot didn't matter to me
until that foot stepped on my neck

"Out of the Concrete a Rose Grew"

Stanza (1)

Out of the concrete a rose grew, who knew
I would be chosen to grow and prosper despite my struggles
Growing up in Reserve, God earmarked me out of a few
I was guilty of my sins, filthy within
I migrated to the Projects, developed a toxic
cultural behavior pattern and prospective
This mindset was forged on me undetected
I established an arrogantly inferior complex
In context, I lectured myself on how to be a super predator, a savage
Neglecting my precious value as a Man of God
Sarah Jean raise me
I grew up in the streets, took the wrong turn, no turning back
Deceptive prospective of what a man should be, fatherless boy
I Partook in the Black underclass
I became the invisible man
I possessed no plan to succeed outside of East 14th
I went to Fifth Ward Elementary
My teachers preached to me to get an education, but
they didn't educate me beyond what I see
When I go outside I see death, mothers cry not having food to
eat, young brothers hustle to make money so they can bypass
waiting on food stamps and make sure there is steaks to eat
Cops harass you for nothing, living in the fabric of racism,
A place from the 1850s where blacks couldn't walk and hang
Out of the concrete a rose grew, who knew
God would choose me out of a few

Who knew, East 14th Street would house a king
My surroundings and environment didn't crown me with a ring
It taught me to survive by operating in a poverty state of mind
I had to go up-state
To educate the king who lived like project kid
I'm never ashamed, of where I lived
Out of the concrete a rose grew
Let's put one plus one together, which equals two
I'm from the hood, but intelligent as the white man
Matter of fact, a Godly Man who is smarter, here is the proof
Let's laugh
I was unemployed, indulged in crime, impoverished, an uneducated fool
Oxymoronic, the way my life is curtail to match the fool who seem wise
It's a disgrace the way I suppressed my greatness in a disguise
I took pride in the way I walked this path of destruction
Selling drugs, robbing and shooting people, my own kind,
I was out of my mind
Rewind, I didn't take mental health serious until I did time, in prison
It took a prison sentence to unleash me into my
purpose, train me for the mission
Rescuing my people out of Egypt
Out of Mental Slavery, enslaved to passions of the world
Rescue my people from the prison of being in one place living as the victim
Save the youth who look like me from the schoolhouse
Because the pipeline is from the schoolhouse
to the Criminal Justice System
Did I mention, one in every four black boys will enter the system
We must end this, Let's stop it
I came to bring light to the blind and preach to the captives

I went to prison, to get my law degree
Just so I can make some legal noise and gain my hearing
I learnt my history and captured the Hand of God
Who called me since I was little boy
I lost my moms and sister on this journey
My pops gave up, but God saved us
Out of the concrete a rose grew
Who knew
A little black boy would grow
Who knew
He would be picked out of a few
Young Blacks Educated would come true
Heavenly Father, you gave me a vision
I trust you to fulfill it
Out of the concrete a rose grew

This Poem is dedicated to my sister, Bridgett K. Alexander (Queen B) who pasted away in 2021, at the age of 26. Bridgett was very special to me and many others being the youngest sibling out of the four of us. I love you and will never allow your legacy to die.

"Bridgett's Efflorescence"

Stanza (1)

Bridgett was an effusion of positive energy,
Her life symbolized efflorescence,
She was pregnant with potential
Her elegance was electrical,
She was kind and passionate
Her insomnia for defying the obstacles and odds against her,
inspired and encouraged you to move forward on your worst day
Her aura gave you a sense of royalty she possessed
Her beauty radiated like the sun
She was patient and loving
She was grateful for opportunity, when it presented itself,
Gifted with thinking
Her fortitude enabled someone to stand in awed of greatness
She was profound and magnificence in her own way
She was a mother before she birthed Rosie

Her motherly charm displayed itself
As she cared for others when they needed it most
She was loyal and true to herself
The commitment she possessed to being a Queen
Uplifted many to transform into the best version of themselves
She inspired me to keep going
She taught me what it meant to be dedicated to your goals
If I could bring you back
I would say
You're a legend
You're a great who paved the way
I know you dancing with Sarah Jean, Rose,
and Tee Barber at Heaven's Gate
I know you waiting for me
Her last words to me were, "I Am My Brother's Keeper?"
She echoed Cain's words from the Bible
But she would tell me, "Yes, I Am My Brother's Keeper!"
Today and Always, I will say, "Yes, I Am My Sister's Keeper"
Yes, I am!
I will forever miss you and allow you to live through me
Your Brother Kevin X

Acknowledgements

I would like to express my most sincere thanks to the following:

First and foremost, I want to thank and give all glory, honor and praise to my God and Savior, Jesus (Yahshua) the Messiah, who gifted me with the talent to write these poetic rhymes during one of the most difficult experiences I ever dealt with as a child transitioning to a man. Thank God for allowing me to discover the most precious gift known to man –Jesus Christ, my Lord and Savior. Through the knowledge of Christ, I know myself. Thank God for giving me the grace and strength to overcome situations I thought would engulf me.

I give all glory to God for my Mother, Sarah Jean Flowers Alexander, who passed away March 27, 2020 from Covid-19. She implanted so much wisdom and knowledge into me. There were many jewels she imparted and dispensed through both word and deed. She truly is the reason I am the man I am today. God bless her soul. Jesus finally got his bride, so Mama dance with Him!

I want to acknowledge my father, Kevin Alexander, Sr., who gave his all being the best man he could be. Pops, I love you.

Tee Cheryl, I love you for being there for me when Moms and Bridgett passed. I thank you for stepping up keeping the family together.

To my beloved sisters: Chassidy Smith, Rachael, Kimberly and Bridgett Alexander (Bridgett passed away 4/2/2021). My beautiful black queens, I love you so much and it has been a blessing being a brother to you.

To my nieces and nephews: Ca'hara, Bunny, Ray' Lynn, Rosie, Kingston, Kayla, Lo, Lil Ron, and Isiah ("Pa"). God gifted humanity with His greatest treasure –children. I love you so much, and this book is specifically dedicated to you.

Thank God for my Aunt Ann, (My second Mom, Friend and Book Agent) and Uncle Jerry. They have inspired and encouraged me along the way to stay focused no matter what I have faced. You believed in me when no one else did. You gave me true (agape) love and sincere encouragement at my darkest hour. Your love propelled me on days when my heart was failing me.

Thank God for Sherman Singleton ("Pus Head"), who inspired and encouraged me to write this book. He assisted me in the editorial process of this book.

I want to thank my brothers who motivated me through the storm to keep being great no matter what I faced. Here all my brothers I want to shout out:

Andre Randolph, Smitty, Ronald "Pencil" Marshall, Juan, Deneil, Faheem, Biggie, Jules, Dougie, Isiah, Pastor Mike, Gary, Swamp, Solo, Tootie, Tweet, Potato my brother, Olajuwon "Lot", Detrick my best friend and day-one brother, Marty "Boss", Black, Kyle, Jamesray my cousin, Big Buff, A.C., Tiger my brother from "225", Pastor Tate, and Dominique Fairley ("Bro. D"); who also assisted me in editing this book, my Brother-in-Christ.

Reginald Harris ("VL"), my Brother-in-Christ who encouraged and uplifted me back into a stronger relationship with God. I thank you for that. Many times you expressed truth to me when I didn't want to hear it and encouraged me to stay focus when I felt like I was losing it. I have much love for you.

I want to acknowledge my girlfriend, Crystal Simmons, who made a lot of this possible doing a lot of ground work on this project helping me bring this idea to life. I love and appreciate you.

Lastly, I like to acknowledge everyone who played a key role in my life. Everyone that assisted me in bettering myself while in prison. All Glory to God for always making a way out of no way and giving me the strength and wisdom to be an overcomer.

About the Author

Born to Kevin Sr. and Sarah Jean Alexander, Kevin Alexander, Jr. (Kevin X) made landing onto earth on November 1st of 1993. He was raised in Reserve, Louisiana, which is in close proximity to New Orleans, Louisiana. Kevin endured a hard life while growing up facing many obstacles and adversities. Growing up, Kevin lived in a neighborhood that was drug infested, plagued by violent crime, and was subpar socio-economically. Kevin's neighborhood was located on East 14th Street. Geographically, East 14th street aligns with East 13th Street (an area infested with inequity) –the Reserve Housing Authority, better known as the Reserve Projects.

Despite his attempt seeking to not be a product of his environment, Kevin still fell into the trap of being just that. He eventually migrated to the part of the neighborhood his mother warned him to stay away from –Reserve Projects. This street was next to his home, so avoiding this place was hard to do as a kid. Once Kevin began hanging in Reserve Projects and making friends there, the decline was evident. There was no turning back from this consuming lifestyle. He started getting arrested at a young age, in part due to growing up in a dysfunctional home and environment. He became involved in criminal activity at a young age, conforming to the images often glorified. Kevin was attempting, as he knew best, to survive the harsh reality of growing up in the hood. This led to encounters with law enforcement, subsequently causing Kevin to enter into the Criminal Justice System as a child.

At the age of 17-years-old, Kevin was falsely accused and arrested for committing the offense of second degree murder. After 5 years of tirelessly litigating and going back and forward to court, Kevin pled guilty to a lesser offense –Manslaughter. He was hoping to end the mental and emotional torture that came with fighting a legal mountain. Kevin was facing a life sentence if convicted. He accepted a plea bargain out of fear and distress.

Kevin is entering his 13th year of incarceration for a crime he did not commit. He has a legal team who fights day and night seeking to get him home sooner than expected. Nevertheless, Kevin has never given up and maintained hope throughout the years. He has used his time wisely by accomplishing many educational and self-help programs while incarcerated. He has earned two Associate Degrees and three Paralegal Certifications in the past 5 years. The maturity and growth during the 13-year captivity forged an educated young man. He continues to better himself every day and anticipates gaining his freedom soon.

Kevin loves to exercise, read, write and study criminal law. He is an active Christian Minister in the church. He is a Juvenile Advocate who is passionate about obtaining justice for youths in the criminal justice system. He prays one day he can join the fight against an evil system that assists with perpetuating the very problem they complain about eliminating. He knows he will be a man who can be an asset to his community by starting programs for young black boys, educating them about how the criminal justice system functions and what it entails. Kevin envisions sharing his personal experiences to illustrate and teach young men about the different options available to them, outside of what they currently see or face.

Kevin lost his mother and sister in a two-year span. These events have only strengthened and encouraged him to clench tighter to his faith and integrity while in the midst of his incarceration. He hopes to keep his mother and sister's legacy going by continuing to do what's right. This book marks his transition and announcement to the world: Kevin has metamorphosed into Kevin X.

CPSIA information can be obtained
at www.ICGtesting.com
Printed in the USA
BVHW040820080523
663770BV00002B/20